The Story of Prairie Rose

based on a Sioux Myth

retold by Michael Sandler
illustrated by Joanne Friar

 **Harcourt**
SCHOOL PUBLISHERS

D1798505

Printed in China

ISBN 10:   0-15-377414-2
ISBN 13:   978-0-15-377414-0

Ordering Options
ISBN 10:   0-15-377149-6 (Grade 5 Collection)
ISBN 13:   978-0-15-377149-1 (Grade 5 Collection)
ISBN 10:   0-15-377872-5 (package of 5)
ISBN 13:   978-0-15-377872-8 (package of 5)

2 3 4 5 6 7 8 9 10   0940   17 16 15 14 13 12 11 10 09

Tommy: Great shot, Jackson. You've gotten a lot better. Soon you'll be king of the city court.

Jackson: Before I moved here, I used to be king of the country court.

Tommy: That's right. I forget. You used to live where? Out on the prairie somewhere?

Jackson: Oklahoma.

Narrator: Winona, Jackson's little sister, approaches the two boys.

Winona: I wish we'd move back there. I don't like the city. There's too much concrete, not enough trees, not enough flowers. I loved the prairie. I loved how it burst into bloom every spring. There were flowers everywhere.

Jackson: The prairie didn't always have flowers, though.

Winona: Huh?

Jackson: Don't you remember that old story? You know, Winona, the one Grandmother always used to recount?

Winona: Oh, I remember now. It's the story of the prairie rose.

Tommy: Tell us the tale. I want to hear it.

Jackson: I'll tell you the story. You'll have to imagine some characters. There's Mother Earth, Yellow Flower, Pink Flower, and Wind.

Narrator: The kids in the school yard gather round as Jackson begins talking.

Jackson: It happened a long time ago. Earth was young. There were no people. The land was not ready. It was uninhabitable. There were no animals on the prairie. There were very few plants, only grasses and bushes.

Mother Earth: I am so sad. My surface is so boring. Everywhere I look I see nothing but cracked earth and dull grass. Oh, how I wish I were beautiful and colorful.

Jackson: At the time, all the creatures that would ever be lived inside Mother Earth. The flowers heard her sorrowful talk. They felt her yearning. One of them spoke.

Yellow Flower: Don't be sad, Mother Earth. You can be beautiful on the surface. I will come out into the prairie and live there.

Jackson: Yellow Flower came out from inside Mother Earth. She went into the prairie. Her golden color lit up the monotonous land.

Yellow Flower: See, Mother Earth? Now you are beautiful.

8

Jackson: Wind was ruler of the prairie. He thought himself dignified when his behavior was really quite shameful. He had a reputation for being rowdy and having a bad temper. He became furious when he saw the new resident in his kingdom.

Wind: What are you doing here, Yellow Flower? This is my place. No one comes here without my permission.

Jackson: Wind blew and blew. Yellow Flower tried to hold on. Finally, she could sustain herself no longer. She withered beneath Wind's mighty gusts. She vanished from the prairie back into the heart of Mother Earth.

Yellow Flower: I am sorry, Mother Earth. I tried, but I couldn't hold on.

Mother Earth: Yes, you tried, my child. At least I was beautiful for a moment.

Yellow Flower: Maybe there is someone else who can stand up to the wind. The endeavor was too much for me.

Pink Flower: I will try. I would like to live on the prairie.

Jackson: Now Pink Flower went where Yellow Flower had failed. Her pink petals stood out against the dull grass and shrubs. Again, for a moment, Mother Earth's surface was beautiful. Then Wind returned, bellowing with anger.

Wind: What? Another flower? You flowers are a pesky bunch! I will get rid of you just as quickly as I did the other.

Jackson: Wind blew again. Pink Flower tried to stand up against the wind. For a while, she succeeded. Then, Wind picked up rocks, branches, and other debris from the ground, hurling them at Pink Flower. Like Yellow Flower, Pink Flower had to give up.

Wind: I don't think I'll be seeing any more flowers trying to dwell in my land.

Jackson: Most flowers were too scared to go to Mother Earth's surface after what had happened to Yellow Flower and Pink Flower. One flower, however, was not. This was Prairie Rose. She was going to try, too.

Mother Earth: Be careful, child. You are my most precious flower.

Prairie Rose: Don't worry, Mother. I know all about Wind. I have heard of his escapades, but I am not frightened. I will be fine.

Jackson: Prairie Rose went to the prairie. Like the others, she lit up the dull landscape. Soon Wind spotted her.

Wind: Another flower dares to appear? I'll blow you back to where you came from.

Jackson: Like the other flowers, Prairie Rose prepared to recoil from Wind's power. Then something happened. As Wind grew close, he smelled the sweet scent of the flower.

Wind: You smell so beautiful. I've never smelled anything that wonderful before. Do all flowers smell as sweet as you do?

Prairie Rose: Perhaps not as sweet as me, but we all smell sweet.

Wind: Maybe I was wrong. Maybe I should not have chased all the flowers from the prairie. I will let flowers live on the prairie from now on.

Jackson: The wind changed after Prairie Rose came to the prairie. He became sweeter and nicer. He no longer wanted to blow away beautiful things. Soon the prairie was brimming with flowers and other plants, too. That's the story of the prairie rose.

Chorus: Good story!

Winona: He told it almost as well as Grandma did.

Tommy: You're a good storyteller and a good basketball player. By the way, is your strength replenished enough for another game? I'm going to win this time.

Jackson: Let me just get a drink of water. All that storytelling has left my throat feeling a little parched!

Narrator: The crowd gathers around the court again. They're ready to watch another basketball game.

Think Critically

1. Why do so many people want to see Jackson and Tommy play basketball?

2. What is the story Jackson tells mainly about?

3. What did Wind not know before coming close to Prairie Rose?

4. How are the characters listed in the second column on page 3 different from the other characters listed on the page?

5. How is the story Jackson tells similar to other folktales or myths you have read?

 **Science**

Fabulous Flower Look up the prairie rose in a reference book or on the Internet. Draw a diagram of the plant in bloom and label it. Then write some facts about the plant to go with the diagram.

School-Home Connection Talk about this book with a friend or family member. Discuss what the story explains about nature. Then talk about other things in nature that may have once been explained by myths like this.

Word Count: 1,109